C0-AVT-785

Cyclops' Eye

By Joseph Auslander

Cyclops' Eye

By Joseph Auslander

Author of "Sunrise Trumpets"

Publishers
HARPER & BROTHERS
New York and London

CYCLOPS' EYE

F-D

26-10 654

TO

MY MOTHER AND MY SISTERS

Acknowledgment

FOR permission to reprint certain of the poems in this book, the author is indebted to the courtesy of the editors of the following magazines: *The American Mercury, The Atlantic Monthly, The Bookman, Books (The Herald-Tribune), The Buccaneer, The Commonweal, The Dial, The Fugitive, Harper's Magazine, The Independent, The Literary Review, The Measure, The Nation, The New Republic, The North American Review, The Saturday Review of Literature, The Southwest Review, The Sun, Voices.*

Contents

	PAGE
Steel	1
Dragnet	9
Inarticulate	12
Elegy	13
Claimant	14
Bough of Babylon	15
Absalom	16
Crow	17
Mirage	18
Silence Is Best	19
Pearl Maker	20
Farewell and Farewell	21
Hill House	23
Deadlock	25
Words for Stone	27
They Said, "You Have Gathered Driftwood . . ."	28
Charity of Frost	29
No Mole, No Worm	30
Fata Morgana	33
Protest	39
Horse-Man	40
Edict	41
I Said	42
Words That Stay Over	43
Moth	45
Bewail Him Not	46

	PAGE
Bravura	47
Condemned	48
Portrait in Acid	49
Diablerie	50
Nunc Dimittis	51
Revenants	52
White Peacocks	54
Nostalgia	55
Mortmain	57
The Riveter	61
Foam Stray	64
So It Goes	65
The Words of Agur	66
Spilled Flame	67
Antipodal	68
Quick-Dead	69
Ultimatum	70
Dark Irony	72
Ulysses in Autumn	73
After Atlantis	75
Dialogue	76
A Certain Pleasant Lady Below	77
There Was a Trial in Athens	78
Mother of Helen	79
Ixion	80
Two That Unlatched Heaven	81
Last Night for No Good Reason	88

Contents

PAGE

If I Am Lonely   89
Sonnets to Amy Lowell   90
Mater Silentiarum   93
Upper Park Avenue   94
Walk of the Worm   95
St. Luke's Summer   96
Seven Wounds   97
Web   98
Business   99
Fog   100
Rain Ghosts   101
Medusa   102
Remember Me, Gulls!   103
Tangent   104
Ghoul   105
Jungle   106
Severus to Tiberius Greatly Ennuyé   107
Gift   109
Knockout   110
Cyclops' Eye   117
Hic Jacet   125

*THIS window is no less than my
Sapient and single eye;
And yet through it I may observe
Duck lifting anchor, watch them swerve
From wind like rock, recoil and curve,
Dragging the black and screaming sky
In their beaks as they plunge by.*

*Blake looked through it and he saw
Duck hustling in a flaw;
Blake looked through it, his eye rolled
On the sun and saw it hold,
Brighter than a guinea's gold,
Seraphim whose coats were thaw
Light, whose hair was curly straw.*

*At this window that is my
Soul I am a summer's fly;
Blake is dust, Odysseus who
Rammed the Cyclops is dust too. . . .
While I stare on you—and you,
Pigs—or angels—in one sty,
Polyphemus stokes his Eye.*

Cyclops' Eye

Steel

THIS man is dead.
　　Everything you can say
Is now quite definitely said:
This man held up his head
And had his day,
Then turned his head a little to one way
And slept instead.

Young horses give up their pride:
You break them in
By brief metallic discipline
And something else beside. . . .
So this man died.

While he lived I did not know
This man; I never heard
His name. Now that he lies as though
He were remembering some word
He had forgotten yesterday or so,
It seems a bit absurd
That his blank lids and matted hair should grow
Suddenly familiar. . . . Let him be interred.

Steady now. . . . That was his wife
Making that small queer inarticulate sound
Like a knife;
Steady there. . . . Let him slip easy into the ground;

Steel

Do not look at her,
She is fighting for breath. . . .
She is a foreigner . . .
Polak . . . like him . . . she cannot understand . . .
It is hard . . . leave her alone with death
And a shovelful of sand.

"O the pity of it, the pity of it, Iago!" . . . .
Christ, what a hell
Is packed into that line! Each syllable
Bleeds when you say it . . . . No matter: Chicago
Is a far cry from Cracow;
And anyhow
What have Poles
To do with such extraneous things as hearts and
    souls?

There is nothing here to beat the breast over,
Nothing to relish the curious,
Not a smell of the romantic; this fellow
Was hardly your yearning lover
Frustrated; no punchinello;
But just a hunky in a steel mill. Why then fuss
Because his heavy Slavic face went yellow
With the roaring furnace dust? Now that he is in
The cool sweet crush of dirt, to hell with your sob-
    bing violin,

Steel

Your sanctimonious cello!
Let the mill bellow!

If you have ever had to do with steel:
The open-hearth, the blooming-mill, the cranes
Howling under a fifty-ton load, trains
Yowling in the black pits where you reel
Groggily across a sluice of orange fire, a sheet
Tongued from the conduits that bubble blue green; if
Ever you have got a single whiff
Out of the Bessemer's belly, felt the drag
And drip and curdle of steel spit hissing against hot
    slag;
If ever you have had to eat
One hundred and thirty degrees of solid heat,
Then screwed the hose to the spigot, drowned in
    steam,
Darted back when the rods kicked up a stream
Of fluid steel and had to duck the ladle that slob-
    bered over, and scream
Your throat raw to get your "Goddam!" through——
Then I am talking to you.

Steve did that for ten years with quiet eyes
And body down to the belt caked wet
With hardening cinder splash and stiffening sweat

3

Steel

And whatever else there is that clots and never utterly
    dries;
He packed the mud and dolomite, made back-wall,
Herded the heat, and placed his throw in tall
Terrible arcs behind smoked glasses, and watched it
    fall
Heavy and straight and true,
While the blower kept the gas at a growl and the brew
Yelled red and the melter hollered "Heow!" and you
    raveled
Her out and the thick soup gargled and you traveled
Like the devil to get out from under. . . . Well,
    Steve
For ten years of abdominal heft and heave
Worked steel. So much for that. And after
Ten years of night shifts, fourteen hours each,
The Bessemers burn your nerves up, bleach
Rebellion out of your bones; and laughter
Sucked clean out of your guts becomes
More dead than yesterday's feet moving to yesterday's
    drums. . . .
And so they called him "Dummy". The whole gang
From pit boss down to the last mud-slinger cursed
And squirted tobacco juice in a hot and mixed ha-
    rangue
Of Slovene, Serb, Dutch, Dago, Russian, and——
    worst——

4

Steel

English as hard and toothless as a skull.
And Steve stared straight ahead of him and his eyes
    were dull.

Anna was Steve's little woman
Who labored bitterly enough
Making children of stern and tragic stuff
And a rapture that was hammered rough,
Spilling steel into their spines, yet keeping them wist-
    ful and human. . . .
Anna had her work to do
With cooking and cleaning
And washing the window curtains white as new,
Washing them till they wore through:
For her the white curtains had a meaning——
And starching them white against the savage will
Of the grim dust belching incessantly out of the mill;
Soaking and scrubbing and ironing against that gritty
    reek
Until her head swam and her knees went weak
And she could hardly speak——
A terrible unbeaten purpose persisted:
Colour crying against a colourless world!
White against black at the windows flung up, un-
    furled!
Candles and candle light!
The flags of a lonely little woman twisted

Steel

Out of her hunger for cool clean beauty, her hunger
    for white!—
These were her banners and this was her fight!

No matter how tired she was, however she would ache
In every nerve, she must boil the meat and bake
The bread——and the curtains must go up white for
    Steve's sake!
One thing was certain:
That John and Stanley and Helen and Mary and the
    baby Steven
Must be kept out of the mills and the mill life, even
If it meant her man and she would break
Under the brunt of it: she had talked it through with
    him
A hundred times. . . . Let her eyeballs split, her head
    swim——
The window must have its curtain!

Lately Steve had stopped talking altogether
When he slumped in with his dinner pail and heavily
Hunched over his food——
So Anna and the children let him be;
She was afraid to ask him any why or whether
As he sat with his eyes glued
On vacancy——
So Anna and the children let him brood.

Steel

Only sometimes he would suddenly look at them and
    her
In a ghastly fixed blur
Till a vast nausea of terror and compassion stood
Blundering in her heart and swarming in her blood—
And she shivered and knew somehow that it was not
    good.

And then it happened: Spring had come
Like the silver needle-note of a fife,
Like a white plume and a green lance and a glittering
    knife
And a jubilant drum.
But Steve did not hear the earth hum:
Under the earth he could feel merely the fever
And the shock of roots of steel forever;
April had no business with the pit
Or the people—call them people—who breathed in it.
The mill was Steve's huge harlot and his head
Lay between breasts of steel on a steel bed,
Locked in a steel sleep and his hands were riveted.

And then it happened: nobody could tell whose
Fault it was, but a torrent of steel broke loose,
Trapped twenty men in the hot frothy mess. . . .
After a week, more or less,
The company, with appropriate finesse,

Steel

Having allowed the families time to move,
Expressed a swift proprietary love
By shoving the dump of metal and flesh and shoes
And cotton and cloth and felt
Back into the furnace to remelt.

And that was all, though a dispatch so neat,
So wholly admirable, so totally sweet,
Could not but stick in Steve's dulled brain:
And whether it was the stink or the noise or just
    plain
Inertia combined with heat,
Steve, one forenoon, on stark deliberate feet,
Let the charging-machine's long iron finger beat
The side of his skull in. . . . There was no pain.

For one fierce instant of unconsciousness
Steve tasted the incalculable caress;
For one entire day he slept between
Sheets that were white and cool, embalmed and clean;
For twenty-four hours he touched the hair of death,
Ran his fingers through it, and it was a deep dark
    green—
And he held his breath.

This man is dead.
Everything you can say
Is now quite definitely said.

Dragnet

DRAG your heart; go deep
   Under the mirage of sleep:
Love whimpering like a most
Inarticulate little ghost.
Let moon water seep, sift
Easily into the earth, drift
Where stone is choked and hard
Roots are resolutely charred.
You will say seven things,
Seven words; wings, wings
Will beat your mouth like birds;
You will fight seven words;
You will say what you have said,
Bleed white as you have bled
Seven thousand times before
Since one word shut a door.
Having spoken, you will break
Star-thread, you will make
Fire freeze, ice thaw
Trapped in the dragnet claw.
What else? You have known
Dull necessities of stone
And your eyes have ached until
Tears were impossible. . . .
Still she stalks through your space
Of music with an old grimace—

Dragnet

Drag your heart; dredge, dredge,
Drive the urgent iron edge
Till the teeth bite below
Strata where no dream could go:
There is much you will find,
Never mind, never mind;
It will be over soon:
Trees inked against a moon
Blotted, blurred, awry in water
Where the moon bores to a spatter
Of writhing roots: that is why
You will twist all awry
As the dragnet gulps through
The black river bed of you.
It will leave you when it's done
Free to breathe like anyone;
Beauty like a rain will rise
Candidly across your eyes,
Wash them clean of little lies.
That is all. . . . And having said
"This hell has not known her tread,
Here her feet will never shed
Pallor like a bright wine;
This hell has no Proserpine!"—
Having said your say, she will
Suddenly brush a window sill;
Put breath on your hair;

Dragnet

Streak flame everywhere! . . .
Always her hand gropes along
The window sill of every song!

Inarticulate

O SPRING, you are pale and fanatic, and I dread
  The motion of your sandals: they
Are strapped with a green lightning and their tread
Is the thunder of water and your eyes are wild grey
And earth is a black womb fiercely tenanted
And the winds sway—
And I am shaken with something I cannot say.

Elegy

FLED is the swiftness of all the white-footed ones
    Who had a great cry in them and the wrath of
        speed:
They are no more among us; they and their sons
    Are dead indeed.

So the river mews twist in long loops over the river,
    Wheeling and shifting with the wind's and the tide's
        shift,
And pass in a black night—and nothing is left but a
        shiver
    To show they were swift.

Whenever I hear a gull's throat throb in a fog,
    Watch the owl's velvet swoop, the high hawk's
        lonely paces,
I think on the heels of him who lies like a log
    And his friends under turf and the rain creeping
        down on their faces.

And my heart goes sick and the hell in my heart could
        break
    To the edge of my eyes for the mates I shall not
        be knowing
Anywhere now though the ice booms loud in the lake
    And the geese honk north again and the heron's
        going.

Claimant

BE what you will: be Christ, be Lucifer—
  Harsh, meek, most tender, most contemptuous;
I must love you: You cannot budge me thus
Nor move the knees of your idolater
To anything less than flame. . . . Retrench, demur,
Bring all your loud alarums to nonplus——
Do what you will: make me your incubus
Or fling me over a star's white bannister!

Kiss whom you will: my mouth shall come between
His mouth and yours; give breath for breath; give cry
For cry; give up your body's white light—I
Shall take them all, my ghost shall intervene;
Even at the last when you yield your soul up
I shall contain you, I shall be the cup!

Bough of Babylon

HOW shall I sing whose harp-strings rot upon
   The old habitual bough of Babylon—
The exile's branch where no tears can appease
The inarticulate and iron trees?
Malignant beauty locked in the cold bough
Never so cold as now.

How shall I sing in a strange land, alone
With time like water dribbling over stone,
And in my heart a small recurrent sound
Like water eating stubborn edges round?
To some grief brings a trumpet's throat, to some—
"O my son Absalom!

O Absalom my son!" O harp as dead!
O flutes for ever choking in my head!
Where is that laughter? Shall I hear again
The dark sonorous music of that brain? . . . .
The bough of Babylon is dripping cold;
This heart is old.

Abaloms

THE jewel casket of a velvet death
  Contains you now, your body and your breath.

Can death be terrible if you are dead?
Dark—with the banner of your buoyant head?

Cold—with the fevered sockets in your skull?
Unlovely—when your hands are beautiful?

The apple dangling by an amber clasp
Provides a golden wardrobe for the wasp.

The jewel casket of a velvet death
Contains you now, your body and your breath.

Crow

TO this cadaverous bough is come
    The sorriest crow in Christendom:
Bitter of eye and blue of beak,
Plumed lustrelessly in a bleak
Acquiescence, huddled in
Torpor gaunt and aquiline;
Gibbeted upon this bough,
What has brought him here, and how,
Inked against the snow and set
In a sullen silhouette?
Let us leave him, let him be
Quarantined from inquiry:
Leave him to his own fierce proof——
Defiant, final, and aloof:
He will have it out alone
And this bough will be his stone;
He will stiffen: his will be
A black immortality.

Mirage

TERRIBLE beauty has cool cloth
    On her forehead, on her eyes;
Never larva of the moth
    Spins here his enterprise.

Lazarus in his death-hood slept,
    Bedded warm in balméd wool.
Till he stirred, till he stept
    Tottering and beautiful.

Let your altar steam amid
    Smoking wine and weep and go:
Christ under his coverlid
    Knew a wound you'll never know.

Silence is Best

I WILL not moan,
    Nor mouth the brave absurd;
Enough that I have known
    Your face, have heard
Your speaking tone,
    Your spoken word.

What is there left to say
    I have not said:
That you are laid away
    With the dark dead?——
Rather that in your day
    You lived instead.

Let the evangelist
    Consider strenuously
His paradisal tryst
    With immortality.
I know how I have missed
    Your walks with me.

And that is all I know;
    Rain streaks the west:
The long rain you loved so . . .
    Your rain . . . As for the rest—
O father, silent below—
    Silence is best.

Pearl Maker

YOU have inserted under my heart
   That sharp and sinister grain of sand
Which, by some salty valvular art,
   Shall one day glitter on your hand.

The word now stinging flesh and bone
   Must patiently achieve at length
Temper more intricate than stone,
   Cohesion of a lovelier strength.

Clouded with nacre, crust on crust,
   Drop by drop, till out of this pain
The moon, trapped in a shell of dust,
   Breaks through—letting the wound remain!

Farewell and Farewell

STILL I think of you and still
    Every sound the whitethroat makes
In the twilight green and chill
    Drops into my heart and breaks,
Tinkles liquid points of glass
    In my blood and brain until
Certainly I hear you pass
    Delicate and puerile.

Never had I known a child
    With the colour of your eyes;
Never anyone so wild,
    Never anyone so wise.
When the branches of the tree
    Antler velvet in the spring
Everything I touch or see
    Takes your wistful colouring.

There was not a beast or bird
    But would swiftly understand
Each little shivery word.
    The quiet meaning of your hand
Shaped for hovering over wings,
    Shaped for talking with the sparrow,
Exquisite with hoverings,
    Cool as water, quick and narrow.

21

Farewell and Farewell

Farewell, places where your feet
   Fell and your laughter fell;
The street-crier in the street
   Puts away his golden bell.
April passionately drums
   And there is a rainy smell
Smoking everywhere and crumbs
   Frozen. . . . Farewell and farewell!

Hill House

(For Frank Ernest Hill)

THIS house in which you live,
  Out of a hill derivative,
Took from hill, tree, and stone
Hill-strength, blood and bone.

Shaped to the hill's shape,
Wearing wind like a cape,
Shaking wind loose like hair
Let down with little care.

Here, in the water-shed,
Water drips from overhead;
When wind and rain quarrel
Water drips in a barrel.

Water went into the nerve
Of this house: that liquid curve
In roof and lintel show
How water washed it so.

It is good that underground
Water makes a homely sound;
As we walk it is good
To feel that murmur in our blood.

Hill Home

At this house let there howl
No hound, no ghost prowl;
Here only let it please
Rain to water white peas.

Here let us dig and rake,
Lay dung for the white pea's sake,
Breathe hard at our work and let
Our teeth taste the clean sweat.

And turn to a beech log spitting blue
Fire when the day is through;
Eat, drink, and go to bed
Like wind and water quieted.

Deadlock

ONE room in all that house was quietly hers:
   Here was her place of kneeling; here she kept
The candles lighted while the family slept;
And here, like other lonely worshippers,
   Occasionally she wept.

All of her windows looked out on the sea;
   Water was like a bird with grey cool wings
   Cloudy over her heart; and there were things
Like seagulls and the thin monotony
   Of their shrill whinnyings.

Whatever in her passionate strange way
   She dreamed or did; whatever work she planned,
   There never was entreaty or command:
"It is best as it is," she used to say,
   "Let the thing stand."

Nobody knew what burrowed deep inside
   Her heart—the hunger, the unhappiness;
   Nobody knew and nobody could guess
The terrible price she paid so she might hide
   What she would not express.

The seasons in their colour came and went;
   All one to her the sunken stars, the sun:

Deadlock

So from oblivion to oblivion
She moved; and it was dully evident
  That all to her were one.

And the brave constellations rise and fall;
  And she whose beauty beggars them is dead
  As though she were the white moon pivoted
On her own death-glow . . . And my heart is gall;
  And everything is said.

Words for Stone

VISIBLY set the seal of death
On her eyes a little wet:
You will soon enough forget
The mist of her mirrored breath.

You will soon enough dismiss
All the lovely ways of her:
She is in her sepulchre;
You will soon forget she is.

She will understand you must
Forget; she will try to keep
Still so that you can sleep
Unoffended by her dust.

They Said, "You Have Gathered Driftwood…"

THEY said, "You have gathered driftwood all
    your years;
We cannot use you: we are moving fast
And doing things so different, so vast!"
This he remembered; now through hot blind tears
He saw the sun rise like a thousand spears;
The slow tide sliding in; a single mast
Black on the sky: and he stood up and passed
Beyond the breakwater and the huddled weirs.

And on the beach the driftwood had been blown
Heaving with the tide and wind. And there
He kneeled . . . a sail swept by . . . he was alone.
A gull flashed white across the broad blue air . . .
They said, "You have gathered driftwood all your
    years . . ."
He groped amid the driftwood blind with tears.

Charity of Frost

LOVE came to me as came to me
 The cool clear meaning of your hands:
So quietly——as quietly
As water when it stands.

It cannot end as all things end,
Grow old and sicken and be lost;
Like water it will comprehend
The charity of frost.

No Mole, No Worm

(For my Mother and Sisters)

THE worm that fed on Helen's eyes
  Closed a golden enterprise;
He touched no peril in those bones
As cold as cold stones;
Nor found that lovely flesh more sweet
Than other meat.

Enough of Helen: we will set
Her ghost upon her parapet;
Delve under death no more;
Shut the curt door:
Let the verdict of the mole
Delicately sift her soul.

O my Mother and you two,
I have found in you and you
Colour which the little dead
Helen might have coveted;
And the deep flame I find
No mole ever mined.

No worm's narrow strategem,
No mole with subtle phlegm,

No Mole, No Worm

Fastens an ubiquitous
Lip on us:
Love without lease or term—
No mole, no worm.

So you, my heart, are no more than
    The mollusc on Leviathan
Seeking a shrewd salvation in
The shadow of that armoured fin,
As you must seek, O brittle heart,
The narrower auspices of art.

Fata Morgana

(For E. C. C.)

(Acknowledgement is made to The Poetry Society of Charleston, South Carolina, for their kind permission to reprint this sonnet sequence which won the Blindman Prize in 1924.)

I

NOT all the vast inconsequence of death;
    Nor the white savour of a dawn whose place
Is washed and stippled to a delicate space;
No, nor the upward trumpet blow of breath
Pitched at a dream, though sinking far beneath;
Nor the dim inquisition of a face
Explored by fingers searching final grace—
Not this, not one of these can I bequeath.
There are some words we cannot say aloud:
We open ineffectual throats and gape. . . .
O Beauty without index, olive-browed!
Black violet night without the old escape!
How shall I bandage flame! How shall I drape
A knuckle twitching in a phantom shroud!

II

Intone no trap of words: these have a way
Of chartering vessels that leak and founder; words

Fata Morgana

Will put a wind along the wings of birds,
Then block their passage to some pale Cathay,
Hissing the while that they and only they
Have strength to spurn the heavy halves and thirds
Of horizontal progress, leave the herds,
Spike gold, split purple, splinter black and grey.
Words can erode velocities of steel
That stagger flashing through a roaring dream;
You reach for syllables to hold to, feel
For words—and they crash by you with a scream:
Words make us grunt and whicker: Circe said
White-honey words—and gave men husks instead!

III

Yet I could bear the hard glazed look that grows
In the grey eyes I must remember still:
I used to fill my hands with colour, fill
Each angry vein with such a fierce repose
That even as I speak it something glows
Under the stiff black slag of love until,
Smouldering through, impatient, frenzied to spill
Over, yearns back the fire that somehow froze.
Always the sting of banked-up passion slides
Like a coiled snake-whip snarling to the heart:
The gesture of frustration that derides,
The accent of the footsteps that depart. . . .

Fata Morgana

And what am I to work with?   Having known
Stars, what can I fashion out of stone?

IV

Let my loud heart clap quiet and be done
With peevish folly and obtuse complaint:
When was that seneschal of dreams a saint
Under the large surveillance of the sun? . . .
And let me finish as I had begun:
Let no half words or quarter phrases taint
The dossier by a dubious restraint;
And put no tears on this oblivion.
I leave no silhouette on some harsh hill
Against the sky, outlined in minor black;
The gestured and theatric imbecile
May fling a studied rose and turn his back:
I only want this body to be still;
I only want these throbbing valves to crack.

V

Is there, then, nothing we can say or do
To stave off what the eyes make manifest?
They speak the thing our lips merely attest,
They speak, and, having spoken, they are through.
Grey eyes glove metal; and eyes that are blue

35

Fata Morgana

Stroke velvet across lightning, veil a breast
With bitterness that will not let us rest
And give us beauty that we misconstrue.
I have in little ways found what I found:
Hope like an old sponge dipped in vinegar;
And that the Place of Skulls is dizzier ground
Than the unsteady orbit of a star;
And that dead love, no matter where we are,
Will search us out and turn our souls around.

VI

To base my feet against your crying flesh,
Jutting my passion like a ladder; reach
Out of this black bewilderment, this mesh
Of nerves the white nihility of speech;
From your small breasts and blue-veined thighs
    achieve
Something that flashes through the blood, transcends
The terror of the impulse to retrieve
In the hot glow that dazzles and defends—
That would let heaven down for me to use;
Loop with a running knot the naked fire
Of constellations; rope stars in a noose
To swing the soul out of a snuffed desire:
The least poor flicker of love's little noon
Is mirrored in the dead pits of the moon.

Fata Morgana

VII

How brave you are! With what a quiet grace
You consecrate our little dreams to death!
No vulgar gaze could guess it from your face,
Your eyes laugh back and even is your breath;
The blue steel of the eyes that used to give
A sullen glory to the stagnant dusk
Withdraws its title and prerogative,
Leaving a blackened shell, a hollowed husk.
A chaos of cold light spills on the ridge
Of a ragged afterglow stabbed by a star:
And Pharaoh sleeps and twitches like a midge,
And sweat is on the palms of Potiphar,
And Cleopatra murmurs names and moans
And I—I have my ashes; you—your stones.

VIII

Had not the sun now breaking in the west
Somehow at dissolution flared up, flung
Light that shivered like an adder's tongue
Into the cell where love had had his jest,
I should not thus be pacing with the rest
Of the proud singers who had starved and sung
And combed their hearts for music and had strung
Bone of their bone with agonies unguessed.

Fata Morgana

Each frosted leaf sputters; frozen trees
Rattle and rub their knuckles together; thin
Cacklings can be heard whenever these
Go rigid and the stiffening locks them in:
Poets and trees freeze from the center, freeze;
But they will touch a star and make it spin.

IX

If I knew what you wanted; if I knew
In some cool single word that it was over:
This thing, this beautiful thing that came to clover
And lifted purple and passed out of view!
Speak. Let it be as clear as two and two,
As sharp and fixed as that; and lay no cover
On it. Say, "Yes, you were once my lover—
And now you are—well—now you are—just you."
Say that . . . and then go on remembering:
That is the unendurable hell! I would
Laugh on the dagger's point . . . sing, even sing,
If you could wrench old roots out—if you could!
But that you must sleep with a ghost and feel
Quick breath against your lids—that cuts like steel!

Protest

I WILL not make a sonnet from
   Each little private martyrdom;
Nor out of love left dead with time
Construe a stanza or a rhyme.

We do not suffer to afford
The searched for and the subtle word:
There is too much that may not be
At the caprice of prosody.

Horse-Man

BELL the centaur if you can;
  Ride the horse, amuse the man—
Still your government must be
Anxiously equestrian.

For the hoofs must have their hill;
Human wish and stallion will
Clash, but do not disagree
Long: the hoofs cannot stand still.

Half-passenger, half-Pan,
Bell the centaur if you can—
Still your government must be
Desperately pedestrian.

Edict

AND so, to quote a brief and lyric friend,
    "We'll to the woods no more; the laurel boughs
Are cut"; the garland darkens on our brows;
And this, if ever, is the very end.
Nothing is here to hallow or defend:
The golden folly and the brave carouse
Are fled; the hawk sits on our banquet house;
Under his talon we cannot pretend.

This is the Edict of our Garden: Go!
The sword insists; the lizard in the lute
Needs not our music. . . . But our teeth shall know
Always the incantation of the fruit;
And at our feet the hiss of heels in pairs
Running for ever down a flight of stairs!

I Said

I SAID, "So much of you is left
  As after bleak toil
Comes the blind, the desperately deft
  Recoil."

I said, "A hatchet hews clean." I said,
  "Offending heart, I sever
You—so! . . . Now you are dead
  For ever."

I said, "I know what I know. I know
  This thing is ended:
Now I can wait till the walls of Jericho
  Are mended."

Words That Stay Over

HAVING watched the wild gulls gather, disperse,
And knowing no better and no worse
What beauty is and the beating of wings in my eyes
And the wind beating in their cries;
Having seen white breast colour and of beaks
The rapid flash and the whistling streaks—
Something in me not to be quieted
Asserts itself like the sound of birds over water and
speaks:

And I say: It would be a simple thing to bear
The weight of death, the impact of despair,
The pressure of contempt or even silence or yet
Endure a clamour I cannot forget;
All this would be a simple thing if words
And water and the bitterly radiant birds,
Gold dark twilight and one throat and one
Face mirroring stars, one mouth murmuring and eyes
still wet—

If all this and all these and the little things
That have such terrible strength could beat like wings
On water once, like wings beating, like swords
On water beating . . . and then no more! . . . But
words,
Words that stay over though the voice is dead

43

Words That Stay Over

To the words; the terror of something someone said
Long ago somewhere and laughed at long ago—
These rust in the brain and grope like a wound that
  has never bled.

Moth

THE channel of this moth is choked with rust:
  Corruption drills a breach
No camphor in the diocese of dust
  Can reach.

In the last alcove of a closeted truth
  The stealthy tenant is:
Regard the ritual of that deadly tooth
  Of his.

Bewail Him Not

BEWAIL him not, the beautiful, the proud:
    Must you insult him with your punctual tears?
The candor of the dust is at his ears—
And all your lamentation and your loud
Harangue of glory pass him like a cloud;
    And shall you rouse him, now the fatal shears
    Click shut, and henceforth curiously he hears
The subterranean ticking through his shroud?

He is no longer hot and bewildered as we;
    Feeble and hot no longer: he is cool,
Cooler and quieter than any of us can be—
    Standing knee-deep in some perpetual pool:
Whether this be his heaven or his hell
Means nothing now—and it is just as well.

Bravura

(For Edward Dewey)

I CAN crow at the thunder hawk,
    Scream contempt to his beak;
Let the loud seraglio squawk,
    Turn white and weak.

Let them scutter to their coops;
    Watch me flapping on my fence;
This red crest never droops,
    This throat scorns impotence.

Though I quake and he scowl,
    His Black Majesty shall know
That for all he may howl,
    I can crow!

Condemned

FROM now on you shall feel me at your side
For ever: you will stand, and I will stand
Parallel with you; you shall know my hand
Narrowly at work upon your pride;
The thumb's whorl in the margin and the wide
Wedge of the leaf turned down and all the bland
Ritual of the sun on paper—and—
From now on I shall pace you, stride for stride.

Though in the custom of your cowardice
You howl for pity, pity there'll be none:
Remembering a certain furtive kiss
Once, in Judea, I shall be as bone. . . .
Dart at my shadow in a slippery hiss
And strike—you shall be striking at a stone.

Portrait in Acid

RATHER than let you know how near you were
To that last devastation of restraint
When you had stripped the plaster from the saint,
Threatened the idol with the idolater—
He damned himself and left you to infer
That he was victim of some tragic taint,
Toying with rouge and brilliantine and paint,
Hating himself to make you tenderer.

It was a trick fantastical enough,
Worthy an expert in aesthetic sham;
If he had only said, "The coarser stuff
Is in me and I am just what I am"—
You would at least have loved a man who had
The power of being magnificently bad.

Diablerie

IT pleased the devil to make you beautiful,
  Appraise you with a black reflective thumb,
Brush in your eyes the brilliant idiom
Of his own sooty speech, and on your skull
The soft soot-colored plumage of a gull;
And in your throat he dropped the honeyed hum
Of Lilith to which braver fools succumb
Than I since Adam found the Garden dull.

It may be I am your predestined ox,
As docile as the fabulous unicorn—
Though not so pretty; fond of hollyhocks;
The first dilemma riding on my horn;
Ploughing the iron of the devil's acre,
Who is my whip as he was once your maker.

Nunc Dimittis

I CANNOT read your purpose, cast
    Clearly into your heart and brain;
I can but contemplate the vast
    Versatility of pain;

I can but turn me from the Sphinx,
    Resume the old Sahara Road,
Find with the lizard and the lynx
    A simple and a sure abode;

Let the mirage and lotos go,
    Relinquish bliss and agony;
And in perpetual desert know
    Palms and water—not for me.

Revenants

MUST it be always so whenever rain
    Rattles a little on the window sill
That I shall hear at ledge and window pane
    The poplar tapping her golden nails—until
The ghosts creep back again?

Is there no peace for you, ghost after ghost?
    I ripped you bleeding forth and watched you go
Staring at me sideways with the most
    Haggard look. . . . Is there no quiet, no
Sleep, you prowling host?

Why do you breathe like thugs who spring a lock,
    Forcing the window of a dream?   What wealth
Stuffs this autumnal heart that you should knock
    So furtively?   Why stand upon your stealth?
Gag the whirring clock?

Enter me decently as you would the door
    Not of a harlot but a friend and break
My lonely crust with me: I have no more,
    Nothing that the paltriest thief would take.
My key lies on the floor.

52

Revenants

When you have done with me, go as you came,
   Erect and unabashed; and tell my dear
Indelible lady that I am the same,
   And that she has no longer need to fear
The poor noise of my name.

White Peacocks

(For E. S. M.)

THESE, who can stretch a white
    Curtain and so shut
The world away from sight—
    Let these austerely strut.

The earth may turn to chalk;
    The rain strike flat and dull:
Still the white peacocks stalk
    Remotely beautiful.

The shaft of level noon
    Feathers no light like theirs:
They step to meet the moon
    Tipping the moon-washed stairs.

Nostalgia

I KNOW, now that the bottom
    Grape tendrils snarl and clog,
It is the hour of autumn
   And writhing fog.

Black meadow mist steams
   In a silver vat—
Something for the bird that screams
   To be screaming at.

Weathered shingles, field stones
   Drip with a dull thud;
Drop water in my bones,
   Water in my blood.

I must get away from here;
   Shanghai men with beards and eyes
Green, and steal a ship, and steer
   To some mad surmise.

I must get a ship and stand
   Parallel with sun and sea;
Touch it with my either hand;
   Smell it foolishly.

55

Nostalgia

I must get away or go
   Daft and yell a crazy yell;
It would be enough to know
   Any ship's smell.

I must get away and get
   Sea dazzle on my skin
Till the glitter and the sweat
   Make my head spin.

Anywhere but here—with hull
   Rank, and rotting deck, and death
Bubbling up in beautiful
   Emphasis of breath!

Mortmain

ALWAYS, wherever there is beauty, any streak
    Or strip of colour on a cloud or in a creek;
Always, no matter where it is, no matter: any strip
Or streak of water or the green glint in a chip
Of rock; a tentative sunrise tinted thin
Cobweb glitter pricked out with a pin;
Noises that put a cool knife through the blood:
Partridge wings drumming in a wood;
A soft wind nibbling deftly at the rain—
All things like these that go out edged with pain
Because of a blind light staggering through the heart—
Always these come and break us and depart.

So that I never know when I say, "Peace
Is with my spirit; I care no longer; cease
To care,"—I never know but then and there
These things and things like these will make me care.
I have grown so tired seeing the rain-soaked streets,
Wet shoes forever trampling newspaper sheets
Maudlin with rain and flattening to the knees—
Oh I have grown so tired of seeing these!
What are you, Life? Are you simply the stale
Smell of water stagnant in a pail?
Can you be broken like broken rain? Or are
You fixed like the frosty metal of a star?
If I could lay my finger on you, cry, "Here

Mortmain

Life, this is you: a bleak and whimsical smear
Down the moist windows of the world!"   If I
Could only nail you down in some keen cry!

I did not think I could endure so much
At your hands: leave the sharp desirable touch
Of women and one woman's mouth that went
Shivery on my mouth; give up the scent
Of skin as delicate as wild white grapes;
The agitated breath; hair that escapes
In tawny whispers; and the eyes that shook
Blue fire; give up every word and look;
The little throaty laugh, the golden bird
Poised in a look and beating in a word.

Life like a leopard stepping, like a paw
Perpetually suspended, like a claw
Hooked in the groaning spirit, what remorse
Assails your nostrils, curves you from your course?
When in your stealthy legend was the truce
Free from the plunging shadow of your shoes?
The sinister velvet and the sultry kiss
I know, and the contemptible armistice
I hardly have forgotten; but I cling
Savagely to my own reckoning:
There have been moments much too vigilant
Even for you; your lungs will never pant

Mortmain

Or purr against those intervals: I have stood
Watch on a hill of stars and under the hood
Of a death's-head moth-moon and have kicked the dew
To splintered silver and have laughed at you.

. . . . .

Night tapped at my temples, at my skin
Night was a needle, a piercing discipline;
The moon a tinkle of ice in a cool blue glass;
Under my soles I could feel the barred worm pass
Hooped in a lustre of rings; earth like a bowl
Cracked with a warm black steam that rose and stole
Chattering into the blood until it hummed;
But my heart was a heavy empty thing, a thumbed
Paper, an abandoned place as black
As a blowing yard behind a railroad track
Where the moon babbles like an idiot
And arc lamps cough a difficult colour and not
A footstep echoes and only a cold ghost comes
Punctually mumbling reminiscent gums.

Yet it was Lazarus April nevertheless,
Called forth, bound hand and foot, to feverishness;
Uncoiling the spiced cloth where death-sweat clings,
Pale spring again after a thousand springs!

Mortmain

No question about its being April again;
The old sweet pallor, the old sweet smell of rain,
Dark dripping noises, bruised earth—God how sweet,
How sweet! But in my heart the deadened beat
Of ghosts on stone. . . . What can I do to work
Clear of that mortmain? Hamlet's feeble dirk?
Or the Moor's pillow and poison? Words, words
Kicking under my heart! As well lime birds
In scarlet wool! No, not that way, not that;
But take the buffet and go sprawling flat
Floored by the dead hand's shadow; draw the knife
Fiercely into the texture of my life;
Make friends; touch hair and eyes; solicit deep
Delight and an opaque impartial sleep!

The Riveter

(For Gustav Davidson)

THE steam-shovels had sunk their teeth
   Through earth and rock until a hole
Yawned like a black hell underneath,
   Like a coal-crater with all the coal
Torn out of her: the shovels bit
The stinking stony broth—and spit.

The Wops went up and down; they spilled
   Cement like a groggy soup in chutes;
They mixed the mortar and they filled
   The gash with it. . . . Short swarthy brutes
They were, who reeked of rock and wet
Lime and accumulated sweat.

At first the work was tame enough:
   Only another foundation like
Hundreds before and just as tough
   To stand under a ten-ton spike.
But it was different when a whir
Of steel announced the riveter.

One long lad of them took the crowd
   As he straddled the girders and hooked the nuts
Livid-white hot: and we allowed
   He was the lunatic for guts;

The Riveter

The sidewalk bleachers yelled as he
Speared a sizzler dizzily.

They got to call him the "Rivet Ruth"—
    That crisp corn shock of gusty hair,
That blue hawk-eye and devil of youth
    Juggling with death on a treacherous stair,
Tipping his heart on a beam of steel
That made his pavement audience reel.

The riveting hammers stuttered and kicked;
    The ten-ton trestles whined in the winch;
And still this golden Icarus picked
    The hissing rivets by half an inch,
Twirled and nailed them on the spin
Out of the air and rocked them in.

And one fine sun-splashed noon he lunged
    Over the stark deadline—and missed!
Swung for an instant and then plunged
    While the lone insane rivet hissed
Him all the way down from truss to truss
And dropped beside its Icarus!

The old strap-hanger thumbed his paper;
    Feet shuffled sidewalks; traffic roared. . . .

The Riveter

Icarus had performed his caper—
   Little New York minced by bored:
Leave the lads with the broken backs,
Soiled feathers and some melted wax!

Foam Stray

(*For Svanhild*)

SHE wears white like a wave;
    When she steps a blue
  Glitter strikes you through;
Her eyes are grey and grave
And pitifully brave.

I have seen her feet drift
    Like water moving on a rock:
Shift and grope over and shift,
    Then stop stock
    Still with a shock.

Earth troubles her; she
    Is Thetis drenched white
    With white gold sea light;
Her heel should be
Set on a white sea.

So it Goes

THE wind has edges honed on frost;
   But although the razor-thinned
Edges cut, the love I lost
   Hurts more than any wind.

Time like a morbid tree
   Shreds the last sick root and dies:
Time is dead for me;
   Space cannot crowd my eyes.

Nothing matters much and much;
   I must say, "Ah well and well,
There are certain things to touch,
   Certain things to smell."

So it goes and so and so. . . .
   I will write myself a letter
Starting, "I am glad to know
   You are feeling better."

The Words of Agur

GATHER the wind in your fist,
　　Bind the waters in a cloth,
Strap the moon to your wrist,
　　Stamp it out like a moth.

The lion, the greyhound, the goat
　　Step in the stirrups of the wind;
The spider spins a cool coat
　　And sleeps in the coat he spinned.

Though all your chains cannot keep
　　The moon and the moth and the hound,
In palaces of purple sleep
　　There also the spider is found.

Spilled Flame

HERE, by your leave, upon this pitiful star
     Where the clandestine worm shares our abode,
We shall enact no trivial episode;
We shall not be as other lovers are:
The passionate chronicle must be lifted far
From those who let the glowing dream corrode,
Rust in the rain as though it had never glowed,
Put the swift torch under an earthen jar.

O lovely minister of light, be quick
To fill the baffled eyes as you would pour
Oil in the lamp, renew the guttering wick,
And send its radiant summons through the door:
If we must be destroyed, let spilled flame pick
Catlike its purring way across the floor!

Antipodal

DUSK that brings the whippoorwill
    Turns my heart to anvil stone
Hammered on by every still
    Tree and tone.

Why should dusty tone and tree,
    Twilight tucking silver hems,
Lift a sudden Battersea?
    Whistler's Thames?

What is there of sound or tint
    Here that I should see the blue
Pallor of a Whistler print
    Of Waterloo?

What have whippoorwills to do
    With the bleak Embankment? How
Reverberates this heart with you
    Here and now?

Quick-Dead

HERE you are dead this many a day and still
In your perturbed bones April plots a daffodil.

Out of your flat black hair her fingers twist
Nervous roots, and out of the blue veins in your wrist.

And from your rain-cooled eyes there goes a strength
Along the stalk, and a light striding up the stem's
    length.

Here you are dead this many a day and still
In your perturbed bones April plots a daffodil.

Ultimatum

(For Leighton Rollins)

SO that, should death press
    Hard green coins to keep my lids
Down, yet this old restlessness
    Would not quiet as he bids,
Would not grow any less.

Too much of the stubborn breath
    And the wing-beat of the world
Would stay till the claw of death
    Relaxed and on his red eye furled
Spectrally the blue-white sheath.

I who never could be still
    Would push through a seam of rock;
Tons of stone and what you will
    Could not hold me under, block
Any heart so volatile.

I would drop a hemlock root
    In a pocket or some rough
Fissure alien to the foot;
    I would break through soon enough,
Nourished on a flinty fruit.

Ultimatum

They who thought me flat and stark
  Would suspect in every vine
Me, my accent, and the dark
  Laughter that was wholly mine
Lifting to confront the lark.

They will tremble—and they should;
  They'll have grim accounts to square:
This bone swift and unsubdued,
  This black and rebellious hair—
They shall make these matters good!

Dark Irony

THIS brilliant animal mirth and this too brief
    Agility of sense in wrist and brain
Must perish in some moon of the dripping leaf
And pass with the duck's wedge and the snarl of rain;
This hand that struck the violin or stroked
The flute to a fever and these brittle cells
Where God gripped Satan will be something choked
And chilled—a pinch of dust, a drift of bells.

What a dark irony that we who leap
Through solstices of song and sweat and groans
Must quit our beauty for a venial sleep
Which the sick buzzard sniffs at and disowns,
And end up spilling in a little heap
To beat at heaven by a door of bones!

Ulysses in Autumn

I WHO knew Circe have come back
  To sink a furrow in the loam;
Left twilights bellowing and black
  For the soft glow of home:
To hear instead of a guttural sea
The needles of Penelope.

Still in my heart the Trojan sack
  Hisses and Helen's beauty goes
Glimmering. . . . And I have come back
  To drink the stale cup of repose——
I who knew Circe and the wine
That turns men grunting into swine.

Can I forget Achilles? Fly
  For ever from Calypso's guile?
The roaring red pit of that Eye
  Drown in some domestic smile?
Cluck at a sweaty plow, who led
The white-flanked stallions of Diomed?

No, for these nerves are iron yet,
  And in these veins, this caverned breast
Echoes the howling parapet;
  The trumpets will not let me rest. . . .
Think you Odysseus drowses so
Who still can bend the terrible bow!

Ulysses in Autumn

The lotos voices call my blood
   Implacable and rumorous:
All night there drums a ghostly thud
   Of feet. . . . O young Telemachus,
Plead with your mother to release
My spirit fevered for the Fleece!

The trees are straining in the storm,
   Spattering gold; and from the sea
The old tang creeps between the warm
   Breath of her lovely flesh and me:
Each dank leaf dripping down in fire
Fuels the dream of Troy and Tyre.

I know it will be some little thing
   Like wild geese in a streaming wedge
Severely beautiful; a string
   Of bird-prints on the water's edge
That suddenly shall crack galley whips
And hurl me headlong to the ships!

After Atlantis

(*For Leslie Nelson Jennings*)

AND have they resurrected Tartary
　　The Terrible? Or out of sand and rock
Lifted the jaguar gates of Antioch?
They who have sacked the starlight and the three
Vaults of a dead Egyptian dynasty? . . .
There is one precinct, one untampered lock
They shall not finger, one cool agate block
Rooted under the cellars of the sea.
Ask of the Atlantean if he knows
Where strain the leopards of his Emperor;
Where sways the stealthy censer of the Rose;
Who wears the garlands of the Paramour;
And where that lonely purple monarch goes,
Along what garden, through what golden door.

Dialogue

"IT is the end?" I said.   Slowly he said
   "It is the end."
  "Then she who was my beautiful pale friend
Is—dead?"
He turned away his head and shook his head.

The years are laggard cattle; the black years
   Emptied of you
No centaur's hoof shall rouse nor all my tears
   Quite creep through.
    Your lids are locked: there is no more to do.

I cannot take your beauty out of my eyes;
   I cannot close
The rumour of my blood though it denies
   April and knows
    The cold kiss of the shears of Atropos!

A Certain Pleasant Lady Below

O WITH what rocking arrogance and laughter
You'll ruffle milord Pluto where he sits
Plucking his outraged beard in windy fits
That shall twitch him most ruefully thereafter!
Scream till the echoes kick at each black rafter
And venerable spiders rub their wits
Quite daft with all this heresy in the pits
Of Hell—with every shriek becoming dafter!

And how the repercussion of your mirth
Shall volley through the grinning corridors
Where that mad motley who have tasted earth
Will pitch their ribaldry until the roars
Assault the kennels and the outer sheds
Of Hell's own mastiff howling with all his heads!

There Was a Trial in Athens

(*For Dr. L. Pierce Clark*)

THEY got you in the end when you had grown
   A little tired of questions: and your scorn,
Old Gadfly buzzing at the ox's horn,
Shot like a brilliant dagger to the bone;
They could not know, nor had they ever known,
The stark unflinching beauty you had torn
Out of the terror of thought. . . . They pressed the
      thorn
Against your forehead, locked your feet in stone.

Was it at twilight that the jailer said
Your cup was ready, sobbing brokenly
Like a sick child, while you approached the dead
With some cool gesture of philosophy,
Leaving to Athens your last recipe—
Two drams of hemlock and an iron bed.

Mother of Helen

WHATEVER she might know and kept concealed
Of the swan's visit singing in her bones—
The swift beak plunging crimson through her
moans . . .
The crash of wings . . . the wound that never
healed—
These were the drama and the dream that steeled
Her swan-split body to the undertones
Of golden agony and made her groans
An eager terrible secret to be sealed.

So when her moon was full and Leda came
Whiter than any moon and turned her sheets
Dyed in goat's milk to darkness with her flame,
Surely her ribs rang steel and hammer beats
And hair whirled like a torch writhing the name—
A ghost-white peacock stalking down dead streets!

Ixion

WHO are you?   Why do you persist
      In strapping me to your wheel?
How can it quiet you to twist
   My spirit on the spinning steel?

The iron and tormented leaves
   Writhe across your jagged gates;
And all my body as it weaves
   Derides the hell it decorates.

Break me slowly, spoke by spoke,
   But at least when you have done,
Let it please you that you broke
   The black wheel with Ixion.

Two That Unlatched Heaven

THE years had done their worst, and these who
were
Lonely enough kept growing lonelier:
The hardening mouth, the dulling eye, that dazed
Indifferent stupor—all that once amazed
Their glittering senses slackened, dangling loose,
Sleep an evasion, work a ghastly ruse.
Still the moon cutting silver and the shout
Of April and the young stars running out;
Still in cold beauty from a tattered cocoon
Uncoiled the moist wings of an early moon.
What gesture, what insidious little trick
Had pinched the soot, had snuffed the candle wick,
Had left them staring in a stony place
With colour ebbing out of each other's face?

There was a time when these two touching grass
Or earth had felt their bodies mix and pass
Fluidly into the green spear or the black
Churning underfoot and then surge back
To them retrieved and altered in some strange
Bright chemistry of change and interchange.
The catch in her breath when she said certain things,
Threading the syllables on twisted strings
Through his heart—what suddenly turned her into
this

Two That Unlatched Heaven

Unlovely woman out of Genesis?
And he, in whom the elements had stirred
Their golden auspices of phrase and word
So that the hills stood in his eyes and he
Poised like a cliff-bound eagle perpetually—
What death had beaten him down till he became
A name she lived with that was like her name?

Easy enough to cry the thing's as common
As dirt, as any man or any woman;
The point is, this particular man had taken
Toll of this woman, had been stormed and shaken
By the trumpeter swans and whooping cranes that
        crowd
Music into the heart when the blood is loud
With love and the hammers of spring. . . . But life
        had pressed
Stone and steel and every stark unrest
Feverishly between her eyes and his:
Prisoners trapped in a mad parenthesis
Of time and place and motion, cornered between
The tongs of swift frustration, slow routine.

So night after night after night she would feel the
    .   fist
Of this grim dynasty upon her wrist,
And stiffen with terror and strain out to reach

Two That Unlatched Heaven

His hands, his hair—and lie there reft of speech;
And so night after night, night after night
This livid incubus that gripped her tight;
And he, a round-faced imperturbable ghost,
Twitching a little beside her in a most
Casual sleep. . . . She'd think of the druggist's wife
In Chekhov's story and it was like a knife;
She wanted to scream, tear all the skyscrapers down
With her nails, batter the perpendicular town
To a pulp: it was a duel for a dream
Between her and the sinister daily scheme
That put him on a train and at a desk,
Distorted love to something sick, grotesque,
Indecent . . . ugh! like nausea. . . .
                                        And then one night,
With late March brawling in the firelight,
Whether it was the smudge on his cravat,
Or whether it was because he coughed and spat
On a gold-spotted log that blistered—she
Whipped out upon him, snarling savagely:
And the wind and the wood and the woman all were
    tongues
Metallic, terrible; and there were gongs
Beating in her temples; and she struck
An ugly short word at him—and as luck
Would have it, he flushed copper, chuckled, said
"Hell, Kate, you've been drinking.   Go to bed!"

Two That Unlatched Heaven

But here was mutiny and of a sort
Not to be clapped in irons by a retort
And with a snarl dismissed. And so the grin
Froze into a half-sneer, saccharine
At first, and then a dark stain as he gazed
And saw a certain woman whose eyes blazed
And whose mouth blazed biting the words out: "Yes!
Drinking! . . . that's right! . . . I have been drink-
    ing! . . . I guess
You ought to know! . . . at least . . . who else but
    you
Could read the recipe of your own brew
Hell-cooked and curdled in the lovely vat
Of your contempt! . . . eleven years of that! . . .
And now, O Christ, the jar kicks off its lid
And his jaw goes agape because it did!"—
The words dug in like nails and his absurd
"Drinking," cut under deep; he choked on the word
"Drinking," stiffening there—the taunt recurred:
"Yes, I have been drinking! Now it's your turn!
You'll drink until you know how it feels to burn
Up with wanting something more than just
Dead walls and clocks with dead hands and the dust
Of stale desires . . . something else . . . if only
To shut out this forever being lonely!"—

He made a heavy effort, tried to speak,

Two That Unlatched Heaven

Failed thickly; she went on in a hard streak,
Lunging her phrases at him like a beak:
"God, don't you see, we can't go on . . . like this . . .
Much longer! . . . and we can't sniffle and kiss
And make up! . . . oh, it isn't as if the both
Of us didn't care . . . we did . . . you'll take your
  oath
On that! . . . I tell you, it's the nasty growth
Stuck to our souls . . . like things I touch sometimes
In the cellar and the contact creeps and slimes
All over me. . . . Well, that's what's happened . . .
  we've let
Dead things touch our hands and we are wet
Rotten with the foul smear. . . . And the one
Thing that mattered hardly had begun
To matter before the fungus got it, the city,
That clever silver leprosy. . . . Christ, the pity!
Well, Christ can take care of it. . . . And now I'm
  going
To sleep . . . perhaps . . . and after that, there's no
  knowing
What I'll do . . . sleep more perhaps. . . . You
  might
Make sure the outer pantry door is tight—
You left the door wide open the other night."

She left him sitting lumped up in his chair,

Two That Unlatched Heaven

He heard her drag her feet from stair to stair
As though she were lifting stones and putting them
    there.
The fire sucked a little, guttered and spit
Once or twice, gasped out.   He looked at it
Blankly. . . . And now staccato on the roof
The wind coughed and the rain betrayed his hoof.
He rose all cold and quiet with a white
Frozen lustre in his eyes, a light
Glittering like ice; and suddenly he'd flung
The doors and windows open, and had sprung
Up the stairs and into her room, and said
"Come down, Kate.   There's a something that was
    dead
That's trying to live again." . . . She pulled a brown
Bathrobe around her and so they started down
Into the splash of wind and as they went
She whispered, "You're shivering."   And he said, "I
    meant
To shut that door—and couldn't—because the scent
Of April wedged between me and the door—
That's what I went upstairs and got you for."

They moved like children stepping through a dream;
Black pools of shadow slid away; the scream
Of lightning clawed at the air and lightning scratched
At their faces as they passed; the whole unlatched

Two That Unlatched Heaven

House and heaven merged until the house
Scampered with the sky like a grey mouse
Scuffling with a yellow footless cat;
The rapid night spattered her bells down, spat
Caressing vowels on one consonant;
The sky was a blue bowl tilted to a slant
Of spilling lines. . . . And under it they stood
Drenched while the downpour staggered through their
    blood,
And they said nothing, and their eyes were wet
Because the storm was beautiful, and yet
They said nothing, only laughed and cried together
Like children stepping through gigantic weather
Toward some adventure, afraid to speak on pain
Of slipping back to yesterday again.

Last Night for No Good Reason

LAST night, for no good reason, I began
    A letter to you on a decent sheet;
Last night, for no good reason other than
The night perhaps, the quiet in the street,
I dipped an ordinary pen into
Some ordinary ink and said, "My Dear,
To-night, for no good reason known to you,
Other than that perhaps the night is clear,
The moon strong and the street as still as death,
I want to tell you—anything, to write
Just—words, to say whatever will be said,
To speak again with no jump of the breath,
To say 'My Dear', and not to be afraid,
To say 'The moon is beautiful to-night'."

If I Am Lonely

IF I am lonely, I am lonely. Let
No charity relent: I charge you now,
Wherever you are this moment, that you set
The placid garland closer on your brow.
The sun hangs like a hawk before he drops
Outstripping his own shadow; and a bird
Pivots on one brief throaty bell—and stops
The anxious echo—and is no more heard.

If I am lonely, what is that to you?
Under this casual moon and under that
Sufficient star the broad world is chalked blue,
The streets are glutted silver. . . . If a bat
Soaks his black leather and his blind eyes through
With silver, what have you to shudder at?

Sonnets to Amy Lowell

(For E. C. M.)

I

SAYING, "She goes forth clean of all harassing"—
I caught nevertheless that recent crying
Wrenched out of your heart at Duse's dying;
And my heart was a bitter lake with shadows massing
Under a sultry electric twilight, glassing
The surface with a sudden terror, flying
Wild with the wild goose phalanx, and denying
Death's stealthy shoe, the gust of his grey passing.

Such was the unbelief and such the aching
Of one who had splintered many a lance in tilt
With you when your brain was a banner shaking,
A white plume streaming, a glittering dagger hilt—
Who now on the black lake's edge sees a hand sunder
The lake and grip the sword and pull it under.

II

People would speak of you as having far
Too little of the central stuff that churns
To a white fire in Keats and instantly burns
The apprehension livid like a star;

Sonnets to Amy Lowell

And yet I felt when you were most bizarre,
Beneath the crackle of colour, the twists and turns
Of your phrase-fury, a sense of desolate urns,
Grey roses, brittle vials of vinegar.

Those verbal agitations and those tall
Minarets of music seemed escape:
You clicked against your palate a proud grape—
Only to taste the sting of golden gall;
And then you slit your veins and spilled their hot
Wine on a white page in a brilliant blot.

III

It was vouchsafed me once or twice to share
Your memorable sessions with the few
Anointed, and to do as they would do,
Toying with lichee nuts or candied pear,
Until a strange intensity made us aware
Of the presence!—and a long thrill ran us through—
And we stood up—and it was vividly You
Saluting your uhlans from the head of the stair!

You talked as none had since the *Cheshire Cheese*
Rocked to the roaring Leviathan: every word
Shot and splintered sapphire, if you please,
And in the velvet havana's haze I heard

Sonnets to Amy Lowell

Occasional sentences as dark as trees
In a sunken forest where there was no bird.

IV

The ravens of the valley will of course
Disturb your faults, according to their kind;
Peck at your candid eyes, pronounce you blind
And celebrate their subtleties perforce;
And the young eagles rallying to the source
Will sniff the speed that left them well behind
And launch their wings, contemptuously to find
Your Pegasus a star hitched to a horse!

Nor will you lack the solemn exercise
Of vestals and gregorian gentlemen
Plucking their harps and humming between sighs
The plaintive panegyric. . . . Until then
Permit me to recall your candid eyes
And what you said . . . and where it was . . . **and
when.**

Mater Silentiarum

(*For Mimsey*)

THE white light of a cloud is in your face,
  Bell tones of wind and water brooding there;
And the hushed colour of your quiet hair
Reflects a tranquil and interior grace.

I strain towards you out of the dust and heat;
  The eagle has his crag below the sun;
  The diver climbs to breath; the fox's run
Is finished. . . . I am hallowed at your feet.

It is for ever enough so to have found
  Silent, unaltered as the Saviour's Well,
  Peace that is deep and inexhaustible,
Touch without contact, syllable without sound.

Upper Park Avenue

THE pavement ringing under my heels is hard
　As bell-metal; and the houses on the street
Stare at the passer-by from their retreat
Of steel: this is the sanctity they guard,
This grim domestic fortress, double-barred,
Where only the anointed and elite
May purr and agitate on papal feet
And your admission flutters in a card.

What are these walls that cut into the sun,
Scissor the sky in little cubes and squares,
Rhomboids and arcs beyond which no blue dares
Penetrate and no casual radiance run? . . .
Dawn, crash into this plaything with your hoof
And send white daylight roaring through the roof!

Walk of the Worm

IF the mattock strike
    Stone or the spade
Bite flint or the spike
    Split rock, be not afraid:
The grave will be delayed,
    But the grave will be made.

Not a pebble or chip
    Must ruffle the bed
Or roughen the lip
    Of the flesh that is fled:
A dream for the dead
    And white linen instead.

The hole must be deep,
    Well-paved and firm,
For the long hard sleep,
    For the walk of the worm.

St. Luke's Summer

THAT summer, as I remember, no rain fell;
  The swamp grass snarled like thread;
  The clay cracked in the narrow channel bed;
There was a livid crust in every well
And a dead smell.

Birds scuffled in the dust and gasped a little
  And died like leaves; light blared,
  Beat cymbals, reverberated; women stared
Stonily at nothing; talk went brittle;
Dogs licked their spittle.

That summer, as I remember, love was lust!
  And even lust recoiled
  From the black kiss, harsh and sullen and soiled.
Two watched a dream sour with a strange rust
And turn to dust.

Seven Wounds

(For Charles Connick)

I DO not think that I shall ever forget
What you said on a certain day: you said,
"Regret no thrust, however you have bled;
Only the coward and the fool regret;
The thing that hurts you is the thing to set
Your cap for!"—and the grey eyes in your head
Glittered—and that day the sun went red—
And you flashed—as I see you flashing yet.

That was last winter. Now another fall
Runs all amuck with colour; and it soon
Will be white winter smoking under the moon;
And my old grief. . . . And I shall then recall
What you said on a certain day: you said,
"It took seven wounds to lift Christ from the dead'."

Web

THE air is webbed with a strict frost;
    And foggily the kenneled hound
Booms; and every noise is lost
    In its own sound.

This is a night when people throw
    Breath like a steaming shadow, pass
In silver silhouette as though
    They moved on glass.

And candles go straight up like strings
    Of pointed light, leaving the wick
Undisturbed, and no drip clings
    To the candlestick.

The ghostly burghers go to bed,
    Citizen and consort creep
From a web of frost, head by head,
    To a web of sleep.

Business

THE panniers of the bee are packed;
   The beetle's jaws are full of meat;
And all the gold that Croesus lacked
   Dusts one dark marauder's feet.

Sunk in the bluebell's womb resounds
   A burly hum of industry;
In every kingcup summer founds
   A feverish little dynasty.

Fog

IN the fog
 Of that December dawn
Man and dog
 Were sucked into mist, drawn
Into a silver bog.

Fog like wool
 Softened the duck's horn;
Cow and bull
 Strayed steaming, forlorn,
Ghostly, beautiful.

It seemed that I
 Had somehow come nearer
Beast and sky:
 I seemed to see clearer
With the fog standing by.

Rain Ghosts

TO-NIGHT the rain is scratching cautiously
And I am sick to death, remembering words
Droned in a dusk of sea-rain and sea-birds
Over the cordial lassitude of tea:
Her small white serious hands, each artery
Distinct and blue; the lemon sliced in thirds;
Her jest about the cream that always curds . . .
And everywhere the dull rain pitting the sea.

Salve the weak little fury of the flesh
With passion irresponsible and shrill:
Remorse will trap you in a bitter mesh,
And still the rain will tap at glass, and still,
Whenever, as to-night, it rains afresh,
You will remember what you cannot kill.

Medusa

I WRITE my sonnets for you, well aware
  That I am less than the sullen drum of bees
To you; and that you care for none of these;
And that it is unlikely you will care:
For still I love you; and the brow you bear
Is pale as death; and you redeem your fees
In dust and vapour and purple obsequies;
And still I love the hissing in your hair.

You are the swift Medusa eyeing stone;
And it is my grim destiny to know
You bitterly beautiful and yet forego
The cold moon of your flesh, your fluent bone:
So I shall always stare at you and turn
To stone for ever—and for ever burn!

Remember Me, Gulls!

THIS is my hour between the flight and the flight
   Of the trumpet gulls maneuvering in half-light;
   Putting their beaks on edge
   With colour; making a wedge
Between the livid twilight and the night.

Soon they will quiet their aquiline throats; and soon,
While the sun crumples like a little balloon
   On fire, their wings will go slack,
   The moon shift almond on black,
And clouds will hook their brooding claws on the
   moon.

Remember me, gulls; remember me, white birds flying
In narrow circles v here the nets are drying!
   By water and wind and the hot
   Reek of the beach rot
Remember me, gulls, cutting to the north and crying!

Tangent

NOW, for a moment, at the end of all,
    As you grin, absinthe-coloured in the glare
Of the spotlight lunging at your teeth and hair
Until the curtain's redundant angels crawl
Down and you take your second curtain call—
I, from wherever I sit, you standing there,
Across the clapping palms and sweaty air
Have held a dream awhile and let it fall.

We will not name it love or lust, nor pause
To pick the poor swift fragments from the floor;
I leave you with your paint and your applause;
The brilliant street is beating on the door.
It matters nothing if a dead dream gnaws
A little; dreams have done as much before.

Ghoul

I SAW the half moon on his back,
   The Great Bow of the stars go slack;
The houses like a fever chart
Shook with the beating of my heart
As I saw Sagittarius go
Slack, and the string slip from his bow:
Gold slid dripping; it went thus
Loosened and illustrious;
Exaggerated pines whose brittle
Branches burned with frosty spittle
Scratched gaps in the blue
Lucidity and let stars through,
Till it seemed the stars somehow
Spat and crackled at each bough;
Shadows with slow angry hair
Huddled on the breathing stair
Private to the moon and there
Roused the reminiscent dead
Chilled, uneasy, visited. . . .
Night crouched, cougar-wise,
A huge cat rocking behind his eyes.

Jungle

(For A. M.)

THAT day it rained, and the day following fell
  Wet and meshed the swamp in webs that glittered
Like a silver pestilence; then a bird twittered,
The tones reverberating like a bell
Of water weaving into a sunken well;
A wind blew; and the blood of an embittered
Twilight streaked the west; a ringtail tittered—
And suddenly the jungle loosed a yell!

The guttural chaffering of the chimpanzees
Shrilled to falsetto and broke off, darkly voweled,
As the howlers beat their barrel chests; the trees
Rocked rain; the jungle roared back disemboweled
Of sound; the moon dripped gold from golden jars;
The night sprang like a black ape at the stars!

Severus to Tiberius Greatly Ennuyé

IN places the water had thumbed the thick sunglow
    to patches
Of oil bloom, peacock flare, adroit black bronze;
And I was a diver, slime-silkened, hot with hot gold
    scratches
Of hammered glitter, slipping from hammered bas-
    tions
Down under dense foam slaver, down under tons
Of weed trash, polyp, down to the cool uncluttered
    deep sea garrisons.

There I blundered through smoke of dim turquoise,
    corroded old
Quinquiremes and galleons and Chinese
Junks and swan ships of Egypt crazy with gold;
Every vessel that had ever brawled with the seas;
Green wrecks, and there went out a glittering vapour
    from these;
And blunt inquisitive fishes vexed their beauty with
    vacant solemnities.

Tiberius, I tell you it would have seriously pleased
    your flesh,
It would have curiously delighted the bone of your
    thighs

Severus to Tiberius Greatly Ennuyé

To go under as I did, pulled through a shimmering
   mesh
Of sun-maddened water, bumping fish with enormous
   eyes;
You would leave your slim dancers, your gleaming
   women with cries
To go under as I did, sliding down a sleek-shouldered
   dream, not otherwise.

Gift

OTHER men have other songs;
    This I have and this I give:
Take it to whom all belongs,
  Single and consecutive.

Heady ferment in a jar;
  Colour storming through the veins;
And the lovely ghosts that are
  You when nothing else remains.

Not a snowbank but is blown
  Powdering to a smoked gold streamer;
Suddenly every Jacob's Stone
  Rouses and reveals the dreamer.

Take these flowers in your hand—
  All I thought, imagined, knew;
Surely you will understand
  Why I give you back to you.

Knockout

A Fragment

(*For Sydney J. R. Steiner*)

"FINAL star bout!" the referee bawls,
    "Ten rounds to a finish! We have—(catcalls)
Over here Kid Ketchel of New York—and here
The pride of Duluth, K. O. Kelly!" A cheer
Slashed through the smoke, ripped the roof off; the
    mob
Shrieked, whistled, went wild; some fan faked a sob;
Then they all booed and baited the Kid as he sat
Nervously jerking his glove-strings and spat
Into the sawdust. The dirt and the din
Were eating him up. . . . His lips licked a grin. . . .
Some roughneck sneered, "Who brung the chorus man
    in?"
Another bird chirped, "Ain't he got lovely skin?"

By now the Kid's feet were drumming the floor;
That crowd of toughs was beginning to roar
For blood: and in the Kid's corner a spatter
Left from the last preliminary matter
Of fifteen minutes of sheer bloodshed—
The Kleig lights kept drilling down on his head. . . .
Then the bell clanked; the Kid sprang cool:
Knockout Kelly tore off his stool;
And that whole bloody house yelled like a fool.

Knockout

The Duluth Demon was all hopped up for a flash
As he swung a bone-crusher and split an old gash
Over the Kid's left eye; and the Kid
Feinted, then shot a right hook that just skid
An inch too high on the Knockout King's ear
Or the quarrel would have ended right then and there.
The crowd went crazy; they yelled and rose
Yelling for a knockout, yanked to their toes
Like a wolf pack snarling at the rumps of buffaloes.
K. O. Kelly dove into a clinch and held
As groggy as hell while the fight fans yelled
For the Kid to polish him off. He chopped
Loose and hooked with a short jab that dropped
The lad from Duluth to the resined mat:
The referee starts counting; the Kelly sprawls flat:
"One—two—three—four—five—six." . . . Mr. Kelly
Rocks himself slowly around on his belly. . . .
"Seven—" He pivots on one knee and spins
Punch-drunk and tottering onto his pins.

The Kid laughs out loud and measures him off
With his left, while the Irishman reels in the trough
Of the squared ring; and then, as the Kid gears to
	crash
The sleep-wallop home, that reopened gash
Over his eye sends a sudden red mist

Knockout

Blindingly down: he flounders, his fist
Fumbles his staggering antagonist;
He plunges head-on to the ropes. . . . Someone hissed
"C'mon Kelly! Kill the bum! Don't let him stall!"
The crowd caught it up and howled through the hall.
The Kid straightened just as the gong struck and took
A smash to the heart and a vicious right hook
To the head. . . . It loosed bedlam: the whole building
    shook
With the pounding of chairs and the yodeling and
    yelling
Of curses, foul oaths, filthy cracks that no telling
Could tell; the banana peel, peanut shelling,
Spit balls, paper darts, gum wads that went flying
All over the place; and the odors defying
The dirtiest adjective; body-vent seeping
Into the stale stench of smoke shifting, creeping
Sullen and sodden through the dank, flat air;
The alcohol cough, phlegm retched everywhere;
The belching; and somewhere the splashing of stinking
Tobacco juice, somewhere the smell of men drinking.

In the Kid's corner the handlers were busy:
Rocco the Wop, Lefty Spanish, and Izzy
Callahan (nee Kaplan) who had cooked not a few
Welters in his day, as clever a Jew
As ever stood in toe to toe with a slugger

Knockout

Or sliced through the strangle-hold of a hugger.
In Kelly's corner the ammonia sponge
Fumed at the Irishman's nostrils; the lunge
Of the towels was lashing him back to a sort
Of second-wind frenzy: he met the report
Of the gong with a one-two that made the Kid snort
And paw at the powdered mat like a bull
Weaving and wobbling in the hot lull. . . .

Then Kelly was on him all primed up to pull
The hay-maker off; he rushed him; the Kid
Back-pedaled, dug under, bored in, and then slid
On the slippery canvas; but Kelly in lopes
Bounded atop him, and, roughed to the ropes,
The Kid grunted as Kelly pumped blow upon blow
That cracked like a piston; he covered to throw
The threat off; the crowd ki-yied; the K. O.
Hung for the crash. . . . But Kelly hit low,
And the Kid caved in, his knees slowly sagged
Under his weight like a buck that's been bagged.
The mob hissed the Kelly; they razzed him and ragged
The referee who, taking one look at the Kid,
The whites of his eyes fishing under the lid,
Raises his arms and starts counting him out;
But at "eight" the Kid groans and, stung by the shout,
Lurches to his legs with the snarl of a beast,

Knockout

Eyes bloodshot and narrrowed and needled, mouth
    creased
On the pain, teeth biting it back. . . . Then the bell—
But not before he had unleashed a short L
That shoot K. O. Kelly like a shot out of hell
And drove the fight fans to their feet with one yell!

They worked on the Kid: his seconds unlaced
The blood-spotted gloves while the youngster grim-
    aced
And went livid when they kneaded him down to the
    waist;
But his stomach was muscled and ridged as hard
As a chilled steel washboard, though mottled and
    barred
With blotches of crimson. . . . Kelly's handlers were
    set
Feverishly on one point: at all costs to get
Their man through the third session somehow; they'd
    bet
He would last that long; and in no mood to let
His battered half-conscious gorilla tin-can
Out of the brawl, his manager began
Slashing through bandage and tape with a pale
Sneer as he pushed the knife under the nail——
And Kelly, screaming with the pain, came to,
Moaning like a wounded animal, blue

Knockout

Ash in his color, a-quiver and wet
With the shock, dripping arnica and sweat. . . .

Then once more the bell foraged with its tongue
Licking at metal: the Kid took the gong
On his toes and was almost in Kelly's corner
Before Kelly, bullet-head hunched for a horner,
Ducked, and butting the Kid in the wind,
Swung him round gasping for breath as he pinned
The lad to the ropes. . . . The arena dinned,
Roaring in his ears. . . . The referee warned Kelly
On the break-away; but no use, for now that whole
    smelly
House was with him, fight fair or fight foul,
As they menaced the referee; and howl after howl
Greeted the Irishman who struck the Kid reeling
With everything but the arc-lamps and the ceiling.

Had he packed a little more steam in the leather
The Kid would never have been able to weather
That insane barrage, for all his tough loin
And tough heart; that recent right lunge to the groin
Was telling on him: it had broken his nerve;
But there's something, when strength oozes out, that
    will serve
For strength: and the Kid, buckling up in a curve

Knockout

Of bicep and bone, shot a crazy left flush
To the button of the jaw! . . . You could hear the
    swift hush
That fell on the crowd as Kelly keeled over
Kissing the reddened mat like a lover. . . .
The referee had minutes and minutes to spare
Till the brute, glassy-eyed, came up coughing for air.

Cyclops' Eye

(For Frank Ernest Hill)

IN that pale hour taken
  Only by the dense preliminary twitter
Of birds whose throats are shaken
As the dew's dust from the leaves
They shake or as the centaur heaves
His flank's dripping,
His hoof's glitter—
So I, slipping with the earth, slipping
Over the sleep-edge between sleep
And waking when the eyelids keep
The worn seams of their web from ripping,
Hung suspended in a dream
As the spider hangs, and in that station holds
Outstretched the groined arch that would seem
To hold him, held and was held in seven folds
Of a staring scheme.

I saw with the heart's throbbing centre (an Eye
That did not see so much as feel)
Tremendously the whirlpool stream
Of men and motors boiling by
Out of a cauldron of steam and steel
Into a cauldron of steel and steam;
I stood at the crossroads of the world

117

Cyclops' Eye

And watched with my heart the street
Churn traffic like a black surf, beat
With shoes and sticks and hands and feet;
I heard the heat
And the horn's blare, the siren's scream,
The purr of rubber, the wrench of the wheel
Whistled from traffic tower to tower, hurled
Through short spasms of space, twirled
Like a spinning little top
From stop to stop.

I heard a thousand wheels wince
Under the throttle of brakes; I saw
Men and motors crash—the splints
Of windshield glass, the bleeding skull, the raw
Horror of a sagging jaw:
I turned my head away in a sick
Recoil, but my heart was rooted still
Against its will by a massive will
That made it stick;
And I cried, "This is a trick
Played by some grinning Olympian lunatic,
Some lucid imbecile!
Strike me down like a paw!
Only let me go!" . . .
Something said, "No."

Cyclops' Eye

And I saw a rain
Thudding and swirling down
Swarthily on the insane
And splendidly terrible town . . .
And I heard again,
Fogged by distance, twinkling as through a sieve
Of silver, the cool and tentative
Twitter of sparrow and chaffinch and lark
Splashing from wet leaves; and I smelled the dark
Smell of the steaming bark,
Pungent and novel, and the smell
Of young twigs and the yearning earth; and I heard
Bird after bird
Spill silver into a silver bell;
And I knew cattle were standing under the line
Of the living thunder,
Standing under
All the yellow lightning and the fine
White fury of water because I could smell the kine,
And my nostrils dilated, drinking the beevish wine;
And somewhere near at hand the shrill
Exultant snuffle of horses on a hill
And the good grunt of swine;
And the odour of straw
Rain-soaked, warm with dove and owl. . . .
Then suddenly I saw, or my heart saw,

Cyclops' Eye

Machines and men frothing in a black bowl
At the crossroads of the world, and the howl
Of men and machines struck at my face like a claw,
And there was a nauseous rending of wood and steel—
    and a sagging jaw!

And I cried, "Let me go!
I have seen. I know!"—
And heard, "Not so."
And I looked and saw a jungle mocking
The leopard lozenged with gold who had sprung
Into a barrel's spit—
And I fell down with it;
And I heard a trigger click like a death's hand clocking
The second, and I was flung
On the trumpets of assault unlocking
The lion's lung;
And I saw the beauty of the lioness rocking
Behind green coals, bitterly blocking
The last yard to her young;
And I saw the panther when there is no help
Rolling a blind gaze on her whelp
And licking it with her tongue;
And I saw the bengal tiger charted black,
With the blonde lightning on his back
Shot down and stripped, or slung

Cyclops' Eye

Over a shoulder, or in the track
Of his long plunge and lone attack
Left for dung!

And I cried, "For the love of Christ, enough!"
And the wry
Silence came like a cuff
On the soul, and I shook with the rebuff;
And the Cyclops' Eye in my heart glowed:
And I saw a ship in a shouldering sea
Strain at her strength,
And suddenly shudder through all her length,
And spark her doom through the sky;
And I heard the metallic cry:
"Women and children first!   Stand by!"
And I saw the life-boats lowered—and smeared
Flat as you smear a fly;
And I saw some quick little fellow who feared,
Shot down gurgling in his beard;
And I saw the decks cleared;
And I saw them try again and try
Again, but the seas were running high;
And I saw a-plenty jump—and die;
And I heard the ship's orchestra strike up brave
Brass—and the ship went down with her load
Of people and bottles and plates, leaving the wave

Cyclops' Eye

In that place
To receive again, assail, overwhelm, erase.

And I heard the murmuring of all the surfs on all the
    beaches of the world
Boom in the ear's hollow cave, and I cried
"Let me loose now! I have seen how men and ships
    in their pride
Have gone down and died;
I have heard their drums and seen their colours curled
Under like shells—and then heard nothing beside,
Seen nothing but water divide
Decently and close once more and abide." . . .
And there was a chuckling and my heart's Eye was
    turned
In on itself and eyed
Dirty corners there that burned
With many a horned lust, livid spots
That reeked of purple and flesh-pots,
Stamped with the hooves and chariots
Of the Assyrian treachery;
And on the wall a Hand that traced
In the dust and webs the words
"Thus Belshazzar was effaced—
Though not his accusation!" . . . And
All at once a clamour of birds
Filled my heart like a hand

Cyclops' Eye

Filling a hole or like a ghost's
Form flowing through a room:
And I heard a sound like doom
Moving, and I knew the Host's
Breath: "Behold your puny boasts
With the worm in his lodge!
Salute your garrison of hawks!"—

And I could not stir,
I could not stir. . . .
The Voice resumed: "Place-coveter,
Apparel-coveter, look upon
The hawk-thoughts of your garrison!
You that see and hear so plain
Others in their pride and pain,
What is it that lets you kiss
The ikon of your cowardice?
Think you to escape the fault
By exalting me, exalt
Your own forehead, salve your soul
With my myrrh and aureole?
You have looked and you have seen
Man the tool of his machine;
Heard the valves and pistons groan
Mute, and leave their lord—alone
With his feeble blood and bone;
You have stared into your heart

And found your brother's counterpart:
For every stain on his head
You shall bleed as he has bled,
And the dead shall bury the dead;
Now I go—but I release
Your heart to a desperate peace! . . .
And I felt that He was gone
By a gust along the stone
Of my dream; felt Him fled
By a gust upon my head.
Then I wept: my hot tears
Burned my eyes awake; my ears
Heard the shouting in the street
Where the men and motors meet;
And my eyes followed the tall
Blur of light from window-frame to wall—
And that was all.

Hic Jacet

(For Frederick L. Allen)

WITH what narrow words
  Death bolts the door:
Farewell, O lovely birds!
O boisterous earth, no more
Shall I observe the sun
Stretch out on your meadows
In the wind long shadows   .
Like strength! That is done.

When blood like a shout
Shook the forest of my veins
I cried, "You gadabout,
A pox on all your pains!"
I did not know how soon,
Quite, quite deforested,
They would shovel in the lead
And shut off the moon.

And the clouds like clubs
Hammer on the hills;
And the wild twilight sobs
With whippoorwills;
Night is a black hound
At a silver chain
Tugging: rain
Rattles on the ground.

125

Hic Jacet

No more shall I hunt
For the gold-eyed otter;
Never grow gaunt
Again for water;
Never, O never
At the green lakes hear
The toe of the deer,
The tail of the beaver.

Farewell, all bright
Flags and the small
Flowers and the white
Waterfall!
Farewell, all brave
Laughter, all speech—
And the cry under each
Like a wave!

What have I to do
Now with the lips
Of love and the blue
Eyes, the strong hips
Of the girls who go
Erect, confident,
The sweet way I went,
The places I know?

Hic Jacet

They want nothing of me;
They keep the hot tryst;
Gnarled is the tree
Like an old man's fist;
But they cut in its bark
Their beautiful, brief
Passion: the leaf
Drops in the dark.

I can limber my bones;
I can loosen them up;
I Have plenty of stones;
I can drink, I can sup
From the stones in the pot,
From the brew of death;
I can hold in my breath;
I can rot.

I can see how it goes
In the kitchen of this cook;
I can cool my toes;
I can sleep; I can look
Whichever way I please;
I can do what I like;
I can laugh at the spike
That nails down my knees.

Hic Jacet

I can listen apart
To the terrible downward beat
Of the blood from His heart
And the blood from His feet;
I can understand
Why they diced
For the shirt of Christ—
I can touch His hand.

The ant that heaves
Mollecular clod
Till he retrieves
His frail facade,
Is of my house,
Is in my breast:
I banquet the guest,
I flatter the mouse.

If the sow's pink litter
Pull at the sow
Their bite is not bitter
To her somehow;
No less with me
Who suck from stone
The brightness of bone,
The bleak melody.

Hic Jacet

This is my answer
To all who ask—
To Life the Dancer
From Death the Mask:
Though your garlands be plaited,
Though you mince to the flute,
Still the flame eats the fruit
And the calf is fatted.

*A*S though I were to prattle of a debt
    Unpaid, a debt that never can be paid,
So would it sound, so vacant, if I said
"Mouth of the woman that has never yet
Failed to move beauty through me, if I let
Words fumble at the light your love has laid
Against my eyes, you would—" . . . . O tin parade
Storming the stars! Maneuvering epithet!
I shall not even try to say these things;
There is an end to trying and no end
To these: to the bleak levels flushed with wings;
The mercy of your hands that apprehend;
Your lips that by their silences prolong
This desperate serenity of song.